Snap books®

GREEN CRAFTS

Cool Crafts
with
Old Jeans

by Carol Sirrine

green projects for Resourceful Kids

CAPSTONE PRESS
a capstone imprint

Snap Books are published by Capstone Press,
151 Good Counsel Drive, P.O. Box 669, Mankato, Minnesota 56002.
www.capstonepress.com

092009
005618CGS10

 Books published by Capstone Press are manufactured with paper
containing at least 10 percent post-consumer waste.

Library of Congress Cataloging-in-Publication Data
Sirrine, Carol.
    Cool crafts with old jeans : green projects for resourceful kids / by Carol Sirrine.
    p. cm. — (Snap. Green crafts)
    Includes bibliographical references and index.
    Summary: "Step-by-step instructions for crafts made from old jeans and information about
reusing and recycling" — Provided by publisher.
    ISBN 978-1-4296-4006-0 (library binding)
    1. Handicraft — Juvenile literature. 2. Salvage (Waste, etc.) — Juvenile literature. I. Title.
II. Series.
TT157.S529 2010
745.5 — dc22   2009031793

Editor: Kathryn Clay
Designer: Juliette Peters
Production Specialist: Laura Manthe
Photo Stylist: Sarah Schuette
Project Production: Marcy Morin

Photo Credits:
All photos by Capstone Studio/Karon Dubke except:
Carol Sirrine with Liam, 32; Shutterstock/Amy Johansson (chain link fence design element);
Shutterstock/Ian O'Hanlon (recycling stamp design element)

Essential content terms are **bold** and are defined at the bottom of the page where they first appear.

Capstone Press thanks ArtStart in St. Paul, Minnesota, for its contributions
to the projects included in this book.

Table of Contents

Introduction

When you think about **recycling** something, what kind of items come to mind? There are a million different products that can be given a second life. One great example is an old pair of jeans. Chances are you've got at least one pair of worn-out jeans in your closet. Or maybe your favorite pair is torn at the knees. That doesn't mean you have to throw them away. With a little imagination, old and unused items can be recycled and turned into something new.

FACT!

Levi Strauss is credited with inventing blue jeans in 1873.

Go Metric!

It's easy to change measurements to metric! Just use this chart.

To change	into	multiply by
inches	centimeters	2.54
inches	millimeters	25.4
feet	meters	.305
yards	meters	.914

Jean Terms

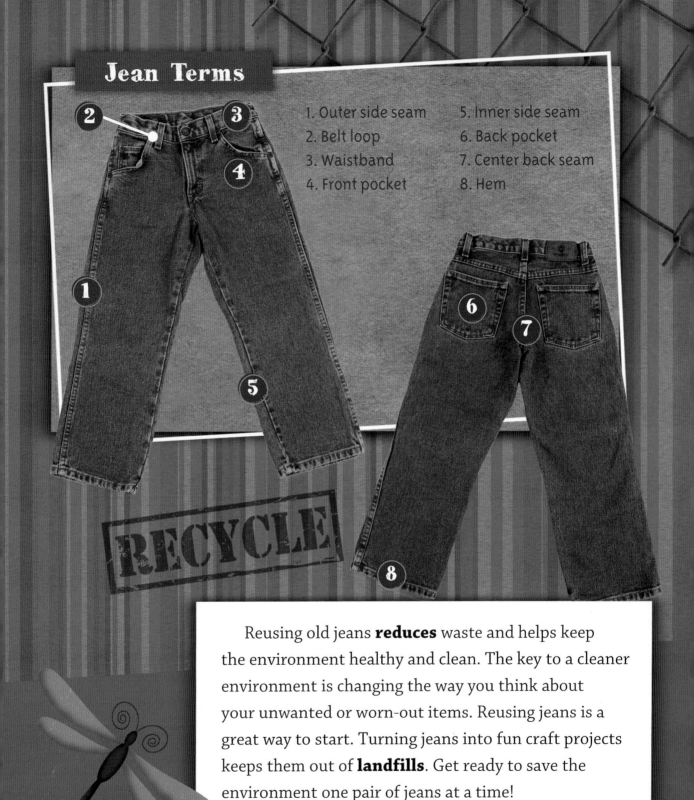

1. Outer side seam
2. Belt loop
3. Waistband
4. Front pocket
5. Inner side seam
6. Back pocket
7. Center back seam
8. Hem

RECYCLE

Reusing old jeans **reduces** waste and helps keep the environment healthy and clean. The key to a cleaner environment is changing the way you think about your unwanted or worn-out items. Reusing jeans is a great way to start. Turning jeans into fun craft projects keeps them out of **landfills**. Get ready to save the environment one pair of jeans at a time!

reduce — to make something smaller or less
landfill — an area where garbage is stacked and covered with dirt

Pocket Magnet

Lockers can get crowded in a hurry with textbooks, binders, pencils, and backpacks. Get organized with some old jean pockets. By adding a few magnets, pockets become a fun and functional way to organize your locker.

Here's what you need:
- fabric scissors
- old pair of jeans
- beads, buttons, or fabric paint
- glue gun and hot glue
- magnet

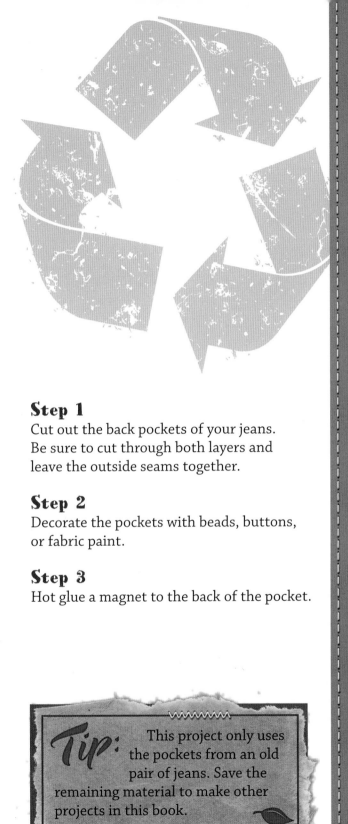

Step 1
Cut out the back pockets of your jeans. Be sure to cut through both layers and leave the outside seams together.

Step 2
Decorate the pockets with beads, buttons, or fabric paint.

Step 3
Hot glue a magnet to the back of the pocket.

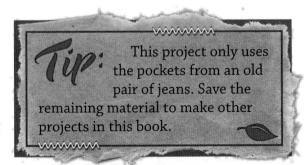

Tip: This project only uses the pockets from an old pair of jeans. Save the remaining material to make other projects in this book.

Dreaming of Denim

You know how comfortable an old pair of jeans can be. But jeans that are too short are anything but cozy. Instead of tossing jeans that don't fit, use them to create a comfy pillow for your bedroom.

Here's what you need:

- fabric scissors
- an old pair of jeans
- straight pins
- needle and thread
- pillow stuffing or jean scraps
- ribbon and fake flowers (optional)

Step 1
Cut off the pant leg of your jeans. Cut off any hem at the bottom.

Step 2
Turn pant leg inside out. Pin one end together and sew about ½ inch from edge with small, tight stitches.

Step 3
Turn the pant leg right side out and fill with pillow stuffing. Make your pillow more earth-friendly by filling it with old jean scraps.

Step 4
Create a 1-inch hem by folding in the material on the open end of the pillow. Sew the hem together with small, tight stitches.

Optional
Decorate your pillow with ribbon and fake flowers.

How to Sew by Hand:
Slide the thread through the eye of the needle. Bring the ends of the thread together and tie a knot.

Poke your threaded needle through the fabric from underneath. Pull the thread through the fabric to knotted end. Poke your needle back through the fabric and up again to make a stitch. Continue weaving the needle in and out of the fabric, making small stitches in a straight line.

When you are finished sewing, make a loose stitch. Thread the needle through the loop and pull tight. Cut off remaining thread.

Braided Belt

The braid is a classic hairstyle that works anywhere from soccer games to formal dances. But braids aren't just for hair. This braided belt is a stylish accessory for any trendy — and environmentally friendly — outfit.

Here's what you need:
- fabric scissors
- old pair of jeans
- thin, colorful ribbon
- masking tape
- tape measure
- glue gun and hot glue

1

2

3

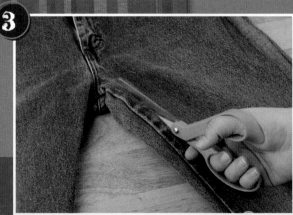

Tip: To make a braid, tape down the three jean strips on a table. Take the right strip and cross it over the middle strip. Take the left strip and cross it over the middle. Repeat until braid is complete.

Step 1

Cut the waistband from a pair of jeans. Remove the belt loops and save for step 6.

Step 2

If your jeans have reinforced outer seams, cut them out of both pant legs. If your jeans have a straight seam, cut a small strip of denim along the outer edges. Be careful not to cut through stitching.

Step 3

Cut out the inseam of both pant legs. Start at the hem and cut up and over the center seams. Both seams should come out as one long strip.

Step 4

Cut a length of ribbon as long as one of the seams. Tape the jean seams and ribbon to a table. Braid the three seams together, weaving the ribbon through with the middle seam. Wrap ribbon around both ends of the braid so the braid stays in place.

Step 5

Use a tape measure to measure your waist and the braid. The difference between the two is how much waistband you'll need to add. Cut the waistband to fit.

Step 6

Hot glue a belt loop to both ends of the waistband.

Step 7

Wrap the end of a belt loop around one end of the braided section. Hot glue the waistband and braid together. Repeat on the other side.

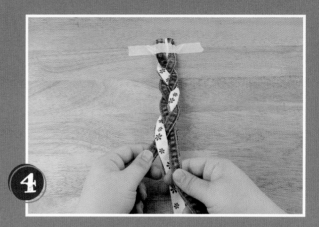

Wrist Wrap

Who needs diamonds when you have denim? With a few snips of the scissors, your jean waistband can become a cool cuff bracelet. To make your cuff one-of-a-kind, just add ribbon or fabric paint.

Here's what you need:
- fabric scissors
- old pair of jeans
- glue gun and hot glue
- needle and thread
- ribbon or fabric paint (optional)

Step 1
Cut the waistband from a pair of jeans.

Step 2
Wrap the buttoned waistband around your wrist. Cut a length of the waistband about 1 inch longer than your wrist.

Step 3
On one end of the jean material, cut the corners into a point.

Step 4
Hot glue both ends of the waistband together with the pointed end on top. Don't have a hot glue gun? Then sew the ends together with a needle and thread.

Tip: Belt loops are great for making matching rings. Just cut a belt loop off the waistband, and turn it inside out. Sew or hot glue the ends together.

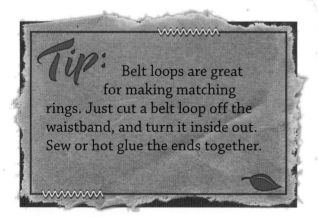

Jean Scene

You don't have to be a Picasso to create a masterpiece. All you need is a pair of jeans, a picture frame, and a favorite photo. Cover the sides of the frame and voilà! You've created a recycled work of art.

Here's what you need:
- fabric scissors
- old pair of jeans
- tape measure
- picture frame
- glue gun and hot glue
- fake flowers, buttons, or ribbon (optional)

Step 1
Cut out the outer seam of one pant leg. Set this strip aside.

Step 2
Measure all four sides of a picture frame. Cut four strips of jean material slightly longer and wider than each side of the frame. Pant legs work best for this.

Step 3
Hot glue a strip of material along the inside edge of the frame.

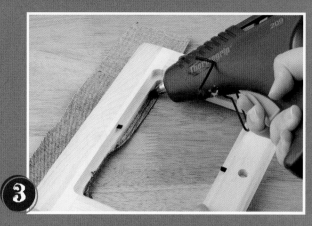

Step 4
Cut the ends of the material strip diagonally to match the corners of the frame. Pull the fabric strip tight across the frame and wrap around the back.

Step 5
Hot glue the strip to the back of the frame.

Step 6 (*not pictured*)
Repeat steps 3 through 5 with the other three sides.

Step 7
Cut the seam from step 1 into four strips the size of the frame opening. Hot glue the strips around the inner edge of the frame.

Optional
Decorate the frame with fake flowers, buttons, or ribbon.

Pocket Purse

Lip gloss, MP3 player, notes from math class. You carry just about everything in your jean pockets. Even if you've outgrown your jeans, you can still put those pockets to good use. By adding a shoulder strap and a little bit of fringe, your jean pocket becomes a fashionable purse.

Here's what you need:
- **fabric scissors**
- **old pair of jeans**
- **fabric glue**
- **pony beads**
- **needle and thread**

1

2

Step 1
Cut out a back pocket from your jeans. Be sure to cut through both layers and leave the outside seams together.

Step 2
From a pant leg, cut a piece of jean fabric into a 6-inch square. Cut the piece into ⅓-inch strips, leaving 1 inch at the top.

Step 3
Glue the jean fringe on the back of the pocket. Cut off any fabric that hangs over the pocket edge.

Step 4
Thread a pony bead on the end of each piece of fringe.

Step 5
Cut the hems off both pant legs. Use a needle and thread to sew the two hems together. (See sewing instructions on page 9.)

Step 6
Sew the ends of the hems to the back of the pocket to form a shoulder strap.

Tip: Want a more colorful shoulder strap? A fabric belt works great. Just trim the belt to the length you want your strap. Then use a needle and thread to sew the belt to the pocket.

Hey Good Looking

Mirror, mirror on the wall, plus a place to store it all. This two-in-one project combines a mirror with a special spot to store your treasures. It's like your own personal beauty center.

Here's what you need:
- fabric scissors
- old pair of jeans
- tape measure
- 12-inch by 18-inch piece of cardboard or matboard
- glue gun and hot glue
- mirror about 6 inches wide
- plastic jewels or ribbon (optional)

Step 1
Cut off both pant legs about 6 inches from the end of the zipper.

Step 2
Cut along the seams of both pant legs to create flat pieces of jean material.

Step 3
Turn material rightside down and lay cardboard on top. Fold material over the edges to make sure it fits.

Step 4
Hot glue the edges of the material to the backside of the cardboard. Cut off any extra material.

1

2

3

4

To finish this project, turn to the next page. ⇨

Step 5
Hot glue the mirror onto the front of the jean-covered cardboard, about 2 inches from the top. Set aside.

Step 6
Cut front of jeans from the inseam to the waistband.

Step 7
Cut along the center back seam from the inseam to waistband. When you are finished cutting, you should have a panel with a front and back pocket.

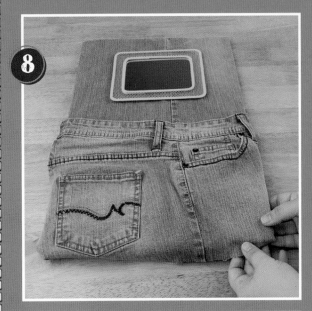

Step 8
Place the pocket panel near the bottom of the cardboard piece so that the material folds over the bottom edge.

Step 9
Wrap the panel around the bottom and sides of the cardboard. Hot glue the panel to the back of the cardboard.

Step 10
Use the second pant leg to cover the back. Cut a section about 11 inches by 18 inches. Hot glue this section to the back of the cardboard.

Optional
Decorate with plastic jewels or ribbon.

Denim Dining

At your next bash, serve up snacks on these decorative placemats. Better yet, save up enough old jeans so your friends can make their own placemats. After all, it's tough to save the environment on your own.

Here's what you need:
- fabric scissors
- old pairs of jeans
- tape measure
- straight pins
- needle and thread
- fabric glue
- colorful ribbon

Step 1

Cut the pant legs off an old pair of jeans about 2 inches below the zipper. Cut a piece of jean fabric 8 ½ inches wide by 12 inches long from each pant leg.

Step 2

Place both fabric pieces right sides together. Make sure the edges line up. Pin edges of the 12-inch side together. Sew the two pieces together on the pinned edge with small, tight stitches. (See page 9 for sewing instructions.)

Step 3

Turn the placemat right side up. Use fabric glue to attach a ribbon border around the placemat.

Step 4

To make the napkin and silverware holder, cut out a back pocket. Be sure to cut through both layers and leave the outside seams together. Glue the pocket to the bottom right side of the placemat.

Tip: To create colorful placemats, try using two pairs of jeans with different washes.

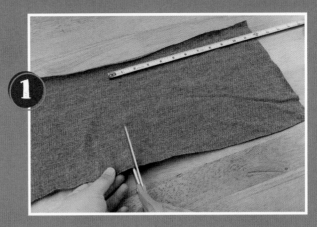

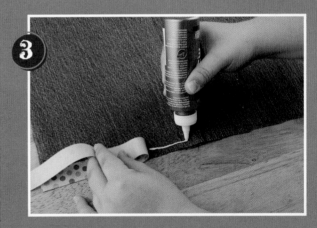

Jean Jacket

From your clothes to your shoes to your hair, you like to show off your style. Now you can dress up your school supplies too. Adding a jean "jacket" is a fun and easy way to make a boring binder shine.

Here's what you need:
- fabric scissors
- old pair of jeans
- 3-ring binder
- pen
- ruler
- glue gun and hot glue
- decorations or
  jean pockets

1

24

Step 1
Cut off a pant leg. Cut along the outer seam to create a flat piece of jean material.

Step 2
Place an open 3-ring binder on top of the material. Use a pen to draw an outline of the binder on the jeans. The outline should be about 1 inch wider than the binder.

Step 3
Cut out the material along the pen mark.

Step 4
Hot glue the material to the binder. Hold the binder partially closed as you glue.

Step 5
Decorate the front of the binder using back pockets or decorations cut from old jeans.

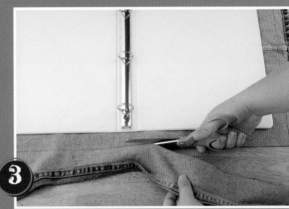

Booty Bag

When a pocket purse isn't large enough to hold all your stuff, you need a booty bag. It's made from the seat of an old pair of jeans. This bag is big enough to fit anything you might need for a fun outing with friends.

Here's what you need:
- fabric scissors
- pair of adult jeans
- tape measure
- straight pins
- needle and thread
- wooden rod (optional)
- colorful ribbon

Step 1

Cut off both pant legs about 2 inches below the zipper. Save the pant legs for the handle.

Step 2

Turn the jeans inside out. Line up the bottom edges and pin together. Sew both leg openings shut using small, tight stitches about ½ inch from the edge. (See sewing instructions on page 9.)

Step 3

Cut two strips of pant leg about 2 feet long and 5 inches wide.

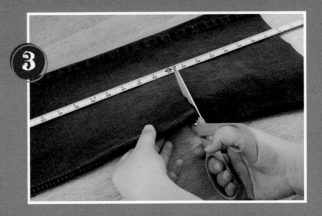

Step 4

Fold one strip over so that the right side edges are together. Sew edges together. Repeat with the second strip.

Step 5

Turn the two strips right side out. A wooden rod or broom handle may be helpful. Sew one strip inside the waistband on the backside. Sew the other strip inside the waistband on the front side.

Step 6

Thread a colorful piece of ribbon through the belt loops like you would with a belt. Tie the ribbon in a knot at the front of the bag.

Tip: Want to travel light? Use a smaller pair of jeans to make a smaller bag.

Green Crafting Facts

Finished all of the green crafts and still have leftover jeans? Donating jeans is a great green practice. Organizations like Goodwill or the Salvation Army accept donations of jeans and other items. Someone in need can use your old clothes and keep them out of the landfill.

Thrift stores are also a great place for you to pick up some new duds. Instead of buying new, shop at a resale store for your next pair of jeans. You'll save money, and the money spent will help people in need.

Denim jeans are made from cotton. Anything made from pure cotton is perfect for recycling into cotton batting. Cotton batting can be used to insulate homes. Call your local recycling center to find out if jean material is accepted. If not, they may be able to help you find a fabric recycler near you.

Cotton crops use 25 percent of the world's **pesticides**. To reduce your impact on the environment, look for jeans made with organic cotton. Organic cotton is grown without the use of harsh chemicals.

crops

Glossary

denim (DEN-im) — strong cotton material used to make jeans and other articles of clothing

landfill (LAND-fill) — an area where garbage is stacked and covered with dirt

organic (or-GAN-ik) — using only natural products and no chemicals or pesticides

pesticide (PESS-tuh-side) — a chemical used to kill insects and other pests that eat crops

recycle (ree-SYE-kuhl) — to make used items into new products; people can recycle items such as rubber, glass, plastic, and aluminum.

reduce (ri-DOOSS) — to make something smaller or less; people reduce waste by throwing away fewer items.

Read More

Craig, Rebecca. *Gorgeous Gifts*. EcoCrafts. Boston: Kingfisher, 2007.

Rodger, Ellen. *Recycling Waste*. Saving Our World. Tarrytown, N.Y.: Marshall Cavendish Benchmark, 2008.

Ross, Kathy. *Earth-Friendly Crafts: Clever Ways to Reuse Everyday Items*. Minneapolis: Millbrook Press, 2009.

RECYCLE

Internet Sites

FactHound offers a safe, fun way to find Internet sites related to this book. All of the sites on FactHound have been researched by our staff.

Here's all you do:

Visit *www.facthound.com*

FactHound will fetch the best sites for you!

Index

About the Author

Carol Sirrine is a former elementary classroom, music, and art teacher. In 1988, she founded ArtStart, an organization that combines learning in the arts with environmental stewardship. ArtStart's ArtScraps, located in St. Paul, Minnesota, combines waste management with art making. In a unique partnership with businesses and manufacturers, ArtScraps collects scraps, overstock, factory rejects, and other items normally destined for the landfill. These products are made available to teachers, parents, artists, Scout leaders, and day-care providers.